Simply Sofia asks, " What race am I?"

By
Brigette Diaz

Dedication

I want to dedicate this book to my loving family and friends, who believed in me and encouraged my dreams, and especially my daughter Sofia, who was the inspiration for this book. I would like this book to be a guide for parents who are only trying to encourage love as I am doing with my child. Teach your children to love one another. Teach your children to believe in themselves.

Thank you,

Brigette Diaz

Acknowledgment

First and foremost, I would like to express my appreciation to Sofia Toledo and Joshua Toledo, whose guidance was invaluable throughout the writing process of this book. Your insights and feedback have greatly influenced the content of this book. Your support and patience have been so overwhelming. Sofia, you are the inspiration for this book, and this is all because of your constant curiosity.

I also want to thank my research team at Amazon Professional Publishing for their hard work and dedication. Our discussions and brainstorming sessions significantly shaped the ideas presented in this book. I also want to express my gratitude to my wonderful readers. Your interest in this book is both humbling and motivating. I hope that the ideas presented within these pages resonate with you and contribute to your understanding of this book.

Thank you all for being a part of my journey.

Sincerely,

Brigette Diaz

I'm home!

"Welcome home, my love!"

Her mom is setting up her after-school snack.
Sofia pulls a chair and hops on.

"Mommy, papi, what race am I?"

Where did you hear the term "race" from?

"At school, some of my classmates asked me what race I was because I do not have an American name and I have curly hair and a dark complexion."

I did not understand
what they wanted
to know.

So I told them
"I will ask my pare
and tell you
all tomorrow."

"By race, you are
an American born
of Hispanic descent.
This means that your mommy
and papi are both descendants
from Hispanic countries
in the Caribbean."

"That is why we speak both English and Spanish."

"Your looks are a big factor in this as well."

"Being from the Caribbean means many cultures are mixed and everyone is different yet the same in a way."

Sofia had a darker complexion because of her mommy and curly hair because of her papi.

Sofia, on the other hand, spoke English just as well as she spoke Spanish. She loved traveling to the Caribbean to visit family and friends just as much as she was excited about living in a big, multicultural American city.

Your race does
not identify you.

"What is important is that we are all equally part of the human race. And that is what really matters."

"We all bleed the same color blood, and we are all from the same creator."

"We look different because the world has to be diverse, which means different in a good way."

"If everyone looked the same, the world would be boring."

I still don't understand what I'm supposed tell my classmates tomorrow.

"Tell them that you are part of the human race by way of your proud Hispanic heritage."

Just tell your friends that you are simply Sofia.

About the Author

Brigette Diaz is a first-generation American born to immigrant parents from the Dominican Republic. She was born and raised in Brooklyn, NY. She has had a love for literature her whole life, and she has passed that love down to her daughter Sofia, who is the inspiration for this book.